Explosion of Dragons

by Annette Corth

Explosion of Dragons.
Copyright © 2007 by Annette Corth.

All rights reserved. Printed in the United States of America. No part of this book may be used or reproduced in any manner whatsoever without written permission from the author except in the case of brief quotations embodied in critical articles and reviews. For information address Annette Corth, 115 Bella Vista Drive, Ithaca, NY 14850, *rcorth@twcny.rr.com.*

Acknowledgements

Some of the poems included in this volume have been previously published in *Footprints Literary Magazine, The Blind Man's Rainbow, Thumbprints, Potpourri, Lynx Eye, Comstock Review, Jews., Senior Circle (Tompkins County Senior Citizens Council), Byline, Knocking on the Silence (an anthology), The Healing Muse, Pegasus Review.*

Front cover artwork, "Explosion of Dragons," by the author and from the collection of Nancy and Harry Katzmann. Author photo by Tony Serviente.

Author's Notes

These poems reflect a mélange of concerns, autobiographical and imaginary, about family, pets, illness, death, old age, love, religion, humor, and language play as well as subjects that do not lend themselves to categorization.

I dedicate this volume to poets Peggy Miller Wolfson, Katharyn Howd Machan, and Naomi Glucksman Levine. Without their guidance and encouragement, no syllable would ever have left my pen.

Author Biography

Annette Corth was introduced to poetry writing in her seventies during retirement as a science librarian. Always interested in words and language, she immediately added poetry to her many interests which include painting, creating abstract stained glass panels, gardening, classical music, theatre, and art movies as well as tai chi, racquetball and skiing in her more vigorous years. Her poems appear in a wide spectrum of publications and she has participated in many readings in Ithaca, New York, where she resides in senior housing with her husband and their geriatric cat.

Table of Contents

Acknowledgements	4
Author's Notes	7
Author Biography	7
October 14, 1927	13
The Puppet	14
The Tower	15
Fear	16
Enemy Alien	18
Table No. 1	19
In the Kitchen	21
Put Him on the Floor	22
Gone	23
Loathed Youth	24
I, Too, Had a Friend,	25
Fallen Friend	26
Cemetery Stones	27
Eleven o'Clock	28
Montague	29
Melting	30
Down Time for Montague	31
My Nose	32
Zigzag Descent	33
Winter	34
Twenty Below	35
Chromos	36
Star Dog	37
No Title	38
Found	39
Worship	40
Religion	41
Picking a Bone with Jehovah	43
GERD	45

Muscles	46
Now That It Stopped,	47
Bag Lady	48
Golden Years	49
What We Have	50
The Scent of Chaos, the Smell of Turmoil	52
Carton Karma	54
Eighth Decade	55
Watching	56
Fear of Abandonment,	57
Post Stroke	58
Hope	59
When I Am Dead	60
Resonance	61
Reunion	63
Pretzels,	64
She Has Left Us	65
Spring	66
In the Plaza	67
One Afternoon in June	68
Shall We Dance	69
Voluptuous	70
Two Fires	71
Flight	72
Vitreous Universe	73
Explosion of Dragons	74
Define Me	75
I Sing a Song to Singer,	76
Lost in the Font	77
Whenever	78
French Critic	79
Picture George	80
Music	81
Cell Phone World	82

Ten Chosen Words	83
Waiting	84
Ashes on Snow	85
Jelly Beans	86
Congratulations on Your Affair	87
Domestic Scene	88
Presents	89
Teaching a Stone to Talk	90
Time Taunts	92
Last Call	93
Afterwards	94
Memories	95
Pearls	96
When	97
Passing Through	98
The Black Door	99
Meditation	100
Sole-Stirring Night	101
Thank You, Dad,	102
William Beane: Redwing, 1888	103
Call	104
Mood Indigo	105
Glitter	106
Romantic Reverie	107
Doing It	108
Ignis	109
What I Put Into The Bag	110
Numbers	111
Dragon's Tale	112
Clangor	113

October 14, 1927

Screams intermixed with animal
moans spewed from the writhing
body. Whiffs of ether,
the clang of metal on metal,
filled the bright arena.
Staccato gasps, terse murmurs:
Losing blood. Tearing.
Head stuck. Forceps.
Desperate push and pull,
then release, fulfillment, a girl.

Half an hour later,
black-thatched, crimson-hued,
I reposed on my mother's chest,
heard (but could not understand)
her first maternal words:
You almost killed me!
I whimpered and fell asleep.

The Puppet

My unconscious father
lay sprawled on the stoop.
Rigid, I cradled his head in my lap.
Rasps and gurgles came from his throat
as I prayed that God would let him live.
That afternoon I lost both fathers forever.

Two men carried his body down the steps,
letting his limp legs drag against the bricks
as though he were a huge puppet.
Fifty years later the memory
continues to fill me with horror.

The Tower

Ocher sand outshone the sun,
contrasted with unbroken blue of sky
and darker hue of unmoving ocean.

Transfixed by the tall white tower standing
at water's edge, banded with deep turquoise,
I saw it slowly tumble into itself
like a drying castle of sand,
collapsing downward into formless ruin.

I knew my father was dead.

Fear

Serenity remains to me unknown.
Fear, ever present, steers my destiny.
Early loss of father scarred my psyche.
Frightened I'll lose any man I care for.

Fear, ever present, steers my destiny.
I dare not love, become closely attached.
Frightened I'll lose any man I care for.
Words of affection always lead to loss.

I dare not love, become closely attached.
My spoken words of endearment might kill.
Words of affection always lead to loss.
I may write or act but not verbalize.

My spoken words of endearment might kill.
Outward restraint mirrors coldness, I know.
I may write or act but not verbalize.
Suppressed inner ardor trembles in fear.

Outward restraint mirrors coldness, I know.
Irrational chains incarcerate me.
Suppressed inner ardor trembles in fear.
Latent tears await sudden desertion.

Irrational chains incarcerate me.
Loving actions, nurturing are my way.
Latent tears await sudden desertion.
I strive wordlessly to tell him I care.

Loving actions, nurturing are my way.
Serenity remains to me unknown.
I strive wordlessly to tell him I care.
Early loss of father scarred my psyche.

Enemy Alien

My mother, transplanted from Russia at age two,
grew up speaking flawless English, but my brother
and I tormented her about her "foreign accent."

She was chagrined to learn the umbrella
of her father's naturalization did not cover her,
his firstborn. We teased the person who
loved us most and accused her of being

"an enemy alien." Embarrassed, she attended
citizenship classes with heavily-accented
greenhorns and would not let us witness
her Americanization ceremony.

In preparation for a vacation to Canada,
we joked that she dare not forget to carry
her "papers" so she could reenter the country.
She saw not humor but cruelty in our words.

To the end of her ninety-three years,
she felt shame at her overseas birth.
Mea culpa, Mom. Forgive. Forgive.

Table No. 1

Momma, do you remember the picture taken
30 years ago of our side, at table No. 1, at
Harry's wedding, before the years jaundiced the
photo and erased all of you, even the bride?
Dick and I survive, but for how much longer?

You and your generation, Momma, all spiffed up,
smiling, now the dust of memory. Dick, grim-faced,
gazing out of the scene, pretending he was no
part of our motley family. Momma, you looked so
tentative.
Did you realize Harry's marriage would be less
than happy?   Did you know already that glaucoma
would steal your light?

Uncle Ben, with a chortle on his face, not a hint
of his impending years of dialysis. And jolly Aunt
Lillian building up her severe diabetes. Dear Uncle
Al, our favorite, full of jokes and delightful tales,
alcoholic, mourning the demise in infancy of his only
child, putting up with his twittering wife.

Aunt Lil and Uncle Marty, no outward clue
to their years of strife.
And patient Aaron, looking glum and tired. Our
husbands do not suffer wedding pictures lightly.
Momma, (I must tell you) Harry married again, hard
upon the death of Elaine.
He is happy, but deathly ill, angina, loss of a kidney.

Momma, I long for your comments, your questions, long to find out what you remember.
I want our memories to reunite us. We loved each other but wasted all those years.
Momma, I miss you.

In the Kitchen

Center of family day and night.
Font of calories, comfort and more.
Yellow table, walls green, fridge off-white.

Dad seated at table head, I at his right.
Mother scurrying through pantry door.
Center of family day and night.

Fragrance of chicken soup. Sight
Of Dad's ketchup, adding gore.
Yellow table, walls green, fridge off-white.

Discussion of trivia with each bite.
Beagle licking spillage on floor.
Center of family day and night.

Odor of mackerel, often a fright.
Coffee time. Mother loves to pour.
Yellow table, walls green, fridge off-white.

Brother and I noisily fight,
Elude every cleanup chore.
Center of family day and night.
Yellow table, walls green, fridge off-white.

Put Him on the Floor

"Put him on the floor,"
I remember asking, so I
could play with the swaddled infant.

Three and a half, an introspective child,
suddenly deserted by my mother,
exiled to an aunt's house without explanation.
Cried whenever my father visited;
he stopped coming. Completely abandoned!

Ten days later new brother brought home
and laid upon the double bed.
I can still see my mother's dress,
a print of yellow, brown, and white,
and my soon-dead grandmother
standing behind her, all smiles.

Mother said I became hysterical
when she appeared.
I recall only "put him on the floor."

Gone

To Harris B. Siegel (April 1931 to June 2005)

Dear brother of many decades,
I beg you to read my mind,
tap into my heart, feel my pain.
You went under so abruptly,
drowned in a septic sea,
had no chance to say goodbye,
left me awash in regret.

Rise again to the surface,
learn how I miss your presence,
your face that mirrors mine.
Your profound love for me
let you ignore the disdain
of an icy, distant sister.
I yearn to have you back,
afloat in memories of our early years.
The undeserved gifts you left
deluge me with waves of remorse.

Speak to me. Give me a sign.

Loathed Youth

I was so glad to leave home,
that place of refuge and revulsion.
Your slovenly ways repelled me.
I hated the dust balls under the bed,
the greasy streaks left on washed pots and pans,
the reek of your unflushed toilet,
the slate gray ring around our bathtub,
the fetid fragrance of unwashed linen,
the garbage fermenting under the kitchen sink,
the rank smell of your unbathed body,
the cigarette butts ageing in every room.

I, Too, Had a Friend,

(for Maxine Kumin)

a curly-haired brunette, pert,
petite, humorful, intelligent.
But life impaled her
on its barbs, leaving wounds
the rest of us would wash off,
bind up, move beyond.

Pierced deeply by divorce,
and wilted romance,
she turned testy, morose.
Drooped by depression, enthorned,
she sat alone in a corner
at my 50th birthday party.
I was too busy to tend to her.

Two days later, Icarus, ignoring
wax and wing, she launched
herself from the eleventh
story. Twenty-seven years
after, I still imagine her delicate
form, arms outstretched, in
billowing long black skirt,
yielding to the greed of gravity.

Was she silent in her descent?
Did her body explode
on impact, release an eruption
of sanguine skeletal splinters?
I want to know but dread to.
Would that knowledge redeem my guilt?
Can we survivors forgive her the desert
her desperate departure left?

Fallen Friend

I watched you die.
My moment of carelessness
let you slip to your death.
I watched your slow descent
and thought I could
reach out and catch you,
save you from the inevitability
of your demise. I did not move,
transfixed by the sight
of you drifting downward.

You landed bottom first,
shattered into dozens of pieces,
each shard full of grace and beauty.
The terra cotta of your interior
contrasted perfectly with
the turquoise of your surface.

As an apology, my fallen friend,
I have painted a loving portrait
of your elegant, broken body.

Cemetery Stones

With grave simplicity,
at times ostentation,
we mark the passing
of the beloved dead.

We divulge bare-bone
biography, display
a brief word or two
of sorrow, give tribute.

We comfort the bereaved,
educate the genealogist,
enlighten the historian,
entice birds to perch.

In a rhythm surpassing
the deliberate cadence
of rain-and-wind-blown erosion,
our mourned replenish the earth.

Eleven o'Clock

Eleven o'clock.
Under the burgundy quilt
we maneuvered for position.
He curled up to my left.
They sprawled atop the covers,
furry, feline forms fitting
in the niches of our bodies,
one behind my knees,
one in the crook of his arm.
Muffled melange of snoring,
sighing, purring.
This is where my heart is.

Montague

He sits and stares at nothing,
neither movement nor sound
perceptible to us.

We laugh, then grow uneasy.
What transfixes him so?
What the nature of feline thought?

He slinks off abruptly,
mission accomplished,
planning his next unnerving
contemplation of the void.

Exhausted by this solemn effort,
he hops up onto the sofa
and slowly melts into sleep.

Melting

A warm spell descends over icicle
fangs and meringued trees.
Whiteness diminishes as if sucked
back to its polar genesis.

The snow recedes to reveal
long-hidden rocks, broken branches,
a glove, discarded roadside trash--
lost relics of autumn.

Montague has shared our home
for eleven years and now appears
gaunt and shrinking, lacking
feline joie de vivre. His bones

jut up beneath loose-fitting fur.
Petting him uncovers vertebrae,
shoulder bones, stark to our touch.
We panic, anticipate mourning.

Time melts away as each winter
marks further loss of our spring.
We collapse in on ourselves, shrivel,
prepare for the last long nap.

Down Time for Montague

With a gift from Morpheus
and an invitation to Thanatos,
we will ease your voyage
from this life to no life.
Aged innards betrayed you,
induced acts beyond acceptance.
Beauty and affection notwithstanding,
you have to go, must leave us forever.

We will remember your green eyes,
the pink triangle of your nose,
the ridiculous caw of your voice,
how your sinuous form enticed
loving fingers to ambulate
among the hills and valleys
from fragile ear to tip of tail.
Farewell, adored friend, forgive us.

My Nose

looked respectable,
neither long nor overly wide.
You could hardly notice its bump.
A blighted romance ended
and needing to console myself,
I decided to have a nose job.

A new nose would spark up
my personality, enhance
my appearance, make me
irresistible to eligible males.
Full of hope, I went for it.

After the operation
(for a "deviated septum"),
I emerged, a nose-splinted raccoon,
a bandit in a deep purple mask.
In time the bruises turned
chartreuse, then faded away.
The debumped nose was
ready for action

A mere ten years afterwards,
I met and married my husband,
who could not have cared less about
the size, shape or angle of my nose.

Zigzag Descent

Snow, icy and crusty,
steepest spot in Utah.
Stiff, scared, shivering,
stuck on Nordic skis,
struggling against nausea
at prospect of crossing
immense treeless, wind-swept
slope in shadow-filled sunset.

I can't. I'm frozen in place.
My spouse, far ahead, turns
and shouts with loving impatience,
"Traverse! Traverse! Traverse!"

Winter

Layers of clouds, pallid
gray through iron-black
fill the January sky, darken
untracked snow, leave no shadows.

Pine trees, splayed and sugared,
guard fields overlain with new snow.
Sole motion, breeze-blown bird feeder.
Only sound, scrapers on glass.

My frigid face rales intake of air,
belies exhilaration felt tracking
atop obscured garden beds.
Occasional dead stems periscope
above whiteness in search of spring.

I empathize with Napoleon's troops,
staggering home from the misbegotten
Russian foray, even with Robert F. Scott,
blundering his way to and from the South Pole.

But cocooned in massive, down-filled coat,
I revel in winter's ice and snow and cold.
This fiercest season garners my every vote:
exciting, bracing, magnificent to behold.

Twenty Below

Not enough light to read the trail map,
no food or extra clothing with me.
The wind swallowed my voice.

Panic yielded to eerie serenity.
Not the worst way to die,
just lie down and drift off.

Undid my skis and blindly trudged
along the invisible trail
to the cadence of creaking trees.

Thought about my husband and friends
vainly awaiting my arrival.
Would searchers come out? In time?

Out of the somber darkness a light,
then a pulsating roar,
the harbinger of my deliverance.

Chromos

Scattered phrases and tangerine moments
electrify my lost thoughts.
Green shivers compound cries
of stemless cataracts on fire.

Mauve voices tunnel through crystal
echoes of future hues as
carillions vie for rainbows
and dragonflies pursue cerise.

Purple dawn encroaches on seven
ancient alpacas. Frost
leaps and laughs reluctantly as
I arise and flee triumphant.

Complex blue webs resound
in infinite conundrums
to listen to frenetic
pineapples of inner desire.

Star Dog

The cosmic retriever
patrols her corner of the sky
bounding from stellar flower
to stellar flower, heavenly tree
to heavenly tree.

In her wake shimmering waves
liberate light through
keyholes of confusion.

She searches for reasons,
the why and how of life
beyond the earth. Alas,
there are no answers.

No Title

I wallow in my shadow
crying out for light, more light.
Swallowed by hovering night,
I see the great unknowable.

Found

In Nature, have I found a savior,
in whose name I rise and slake
all pain in praise of its creation—
snowflakes, mountain lakes, garter snakes,
autumn rain, fields of grain, the whooping crane,
tectonic plates, volcanoes, rainbows,
golden maize, ocean waves, scent of sage.

Worship

I pray to many gods,
one of water, one of thunder,
one of fire, one of laughter,
one of birds, one of boulders,
one of granite, one of dolphins.
I also venerate three of wind--
the breeze that smells of lavender,
the gust that cools the brow,
the gale that thrills with fear--
the only trinity I do revere.

Religion

I, a humanist, atheist, artist
Yearn for the ideal religion, a creed
Would join a community of like souls
Have criteria for spiritual needs

Yearn for the ideal religion, a creed
A church with awesome architecture
Have criteria for spiritual needs
Soaring Gothic, ornate Islamic

A church with awesome architecture
Dazzling, daring post-contemporary
Soaring Gothic, ornate Islamic
Glow of stained glass, gold, gleaming mosaics

Dazzling, daring post-contemporary
Majestic, sinuous calligraphy
Glow of stained glass, gold, gleaming mosaics
Icons of Nature's awesome creatures

Majestic, sinuous calligraphy
Bengal tigers, dragonflies, caribou
Icons of Nature's awesome creatures
Such extraordinary handiwork!

Bengal tigers, dragonflies, caribou
And music, synergy of mighty sound
Such extraordinary handiwork!
Verdi opera, chant of medieval monks

And music, synergy of mighty sound
Russian Orthodox choirs, African song
Verdi opera, chant of medieval monks
Rousing trumpets, cymbals, thunder of drums

Russian Orthodox choirs, African song
O let the spirit tremble in ecstasy!
Rousing trumpets, cymbals, thunder of drums
Evoke tears of joyful fulfillment

O let the spirit tremble in ecstasy!
Loving leaders resplendently garbed
Evoke tears of joyful fulfillment
Flowing raiment, exotic and golden

Loving leaders resplendently garbed
Rites conducted mid brilliant pageantry
Flowing raiment, exotic and golden
Candles, incense, flowers, banners and bells

Rites conducted mid brilliant pageantry
Worship glory of nature, joy of life
Candles, incense, flowers, banners and bells
Message of hope, respect for every being

Worship glory of nature, joy of life
I, a humanist, atheist, artist
Message of hope, respect for every being
Would join a community of like souls

Picking a Bone with Jehovah

Hey, God, listen up. We've got to talk.
But first, let's get one thing straight:
Did we in fact create You or did You
make us? OK, OK, simmer down.
We'll get to that some other time.

Let's assume You **are** the Father
of all creation. Well, You sure
did one helluva rotten job, Dad,
half-ass all the way. Face it,
O Lord, You verily goofed.

If You are so wonderful, so perfect,
how come You made cancer, canker sores,
cholera, diabetes, dysentery and dementia,
TB, VD, and AIDS? What's the purpose
of poverty, pain, pestilence? Why
program people to pursue conflict,
cruelty, and corruption? If You
make something, for heaven's sake,
use a little quality control!

It's bad enough that I can't carry
a tune or dance with grace, but why
lay acne and crumby teeth on me,
slay my father so early in his life,
try to smite my husband with a stroke?

God, You must fess up to some
serious personality defects.
You are drowning in hubris.
With all Your shortcomings,

You have the holy gall to demand
that we kowtow to Your invisible
presence, offer You mountains
of unconditional praise, and
prostrate ourselves in prayer,
begging for Your help to cope
with the crappy cards You deal us.

Why insist that we swear
eternal love for You? Where
in hell is your self-esteem?
With Your irrational wrath,
You sorely need some anger
management. How can we trust
in You when You are so irascible,
so arbitrary? One final question, Lord.
What kind of a god reigns through fear?
You're as shameless as the Wizard of Oz.

Goddammit, I've really had it up to
here with You. Shape up already.
Amen. Amen. Amen.

GERD

Hydrochloric acid, created
by my own gizzard, ascends,
belches out of hell.
When hiatal gate hangs
ajar, incendiary juice
erupts from the confines
of gurgling gastric sac,
seeks a higher life,
fields to erode and devour.

I subdue Dragon's assault
with pharmaceutical sword,
force-feed it tasteless pap,
bore it to quiescence,
then drift into reveries
of tabasco, fried chicken,
wine, chocolate, strong coffee,
cheesecake, limes, curry,
jalapeños, marinara sauce.

Muscles

The heart, beating, beating, fueled
by blood, encased in cage of bone,
pumping, pumping its life force.

The penis, hanging, hanging, fueled
by blood, encased in lust,
rising, rising, pumping seeds of life.

Sphincter, sphincter, opening
closing, opening, closing,
emitting acid, excrement, light.

Biceps, biceps, dwelling in arms,
awaiting call to action, growing,
growing--flex, relax, flex, relax.

Now That It Stopped,

I miss it, long for its return.
Painful, yes, but like
post-storm rainbows,
full of promise and renewal.
I forgot how it started or why.
When it begins, I suffer
the agony, await the
exhilaration that follows.
It sucks up my dreams,
spits out my tranquility,
swallows my marriage.
I fear it. I hate it. I adore it.

Bag Lady

beg, big, bog, bug, bag,
carried by a homeless hag

big, bog, bug, bag, beg,
moving on a twisted leg

bog, bug, bag, beg, big,
limping towards another gig

bug, bag, beg, big, bog,
our nation's missing cog

bag, beg, big, bog, bug,
life shoved underneath the rug

Golden Years

When the gears don't always mesh,
the mind no longer spry or fresh,
seek a word, a phrase, a name
from tip of tongue or whence it came.
Know the face, the meaning, the term.
Was it Donald, fruit salad or maybe sperm?
The more you try to recall what's lost,
the more the memory's like salad tossed.
If you try and try and find no light,
smile benignly, sigh, then call it a night.

What We Have

Between us we have one
hundred fifty-eight years,
one cat, one car, one TV set,
one four-room apartment,
two bathrooms, four closets,
ten radios, three telephones,
one erratic computer,
three children, six grandchildren,
two siblings, one ancient parent,
one nation divisible, ten
prescription drugs, six vitamins,
six table lamps, three floor lamps,
three thesauri, four dictionaries,
four umbrellas, one atlas, two beach
chairs, one card table, four
brown metal matching seats,
one corkscrew, five sauce pans,
two blood pressure machines,
one darkroom, one ad hoc studio,
two hundred and twelve CD's,
forty-seven cassette tapes,
four CD players, one electronic
piano, two recorders, one kazoo,
one bowling ball, two shovels.

We are not burdened by
perfect pitch, the ability to dance,
firearms, furs, 20/20 vision,
photographic memory,
a happy childhood, theism,

jewels, family secrets,
family reunions, motorcycles,
machetes, boredom, blind
patriotism, golf clubs, isolation,
optimism for the future,
a full set of teeth, good posture,
known enemies, national
recognition, rapacious heirs,
stylish wardrobes, alcoholism,
Avon ladies, Jehovah's Witnesses.

The Scent of Chaos, the Smell of Turmoil

Raised ranch house, four bedrooms, two studios,
three baths, office, cathedral-ceilinged living room,
carpentry shop, double garage, sauna, darkroom,
model railroad space, laundry room, walk-in pantry.
Nested on five acres with barn, pond, tool shed, silo,
twelve garden beds, sixty-four trees—maple, pine,
horse chestnut, poplar, weeping willow, grove of aspens.

Stench of stress permeates all. Elderly couple,
tumbling towards eighties, prepares to relocate
to next-to-final resting place--senior housing,
compact two-bedroom apartment. Life inverts.
Insomnia rampages. Lists beget lists produce lists.
Children descend to scoop up desired pictures,
furniture, tools. Reluctant largesse rains
down on friends and local needy.

Odor of despair mingles with reek of fatigue.
Tempers spike. Decisions compete with bouts
of regret and incessant flip of calendar pages.
Chagrin at finding plethora of long-forgotten stuff.
Downsizing rages. Garage sale approaches,
strangers coming to carry away memories.
Fear of furniture not fitting. Excess treasures
outsourced to barns of friends and family.

Mounds, then hills, finally mountains of cartons
appear, fill corners, encircle center of rooms.
Walls become naked, cupboards bare, closets

fill with echoes. The pair struggle to fit
elephant of belongings into thimble
of space. Moving day looms. Bickering
increases. Multiple tasks vie for attention.
Confusion, weariness, the need for closure,
despair they will ever get out alive.

Carton Karma

Acknowledging their senior status,
they pack four decades of marriage
into a tan topography of cartons.

The ritual padding, wrapping, taping,
finalized by scrawled black labeling
of contents, epitomizes their days.

A parade of stuff—clothes, cameras, CD's,
socket wrenches, pills, paints, pictures,
pots—bears witness to their existence.

They laugh and groan at the tedium
of their work, joke about the provenance
hidden by each carton they fill.

The heap of boxes portends in silence
the imminent unraveling of their karma
as the couple nears its final place.

Eighth Decade

> *The hours collapse into one another's arms.*
> *The stories arc over noon and descend*
> *like slow ferris wheels into the haze of evening.*
> *You wish you could stop listening and get serious*
>
> Billy Collins   "Hopeless But Not Serious"

Vigor marked the days of decade number six;
the seventies arrived with caution but verve.
Seventy-eight. The stroke struck and time stumbled.
The hours collapsed into one another's arms.

Embedded in hospital, sun time and star time,
life became IV's, oxygen, blood thinners, double
vision, spinning world, vertigo from hell, vomit.
The stories arc over noon and descend.

His pressure soars and dips. She droops
and rallies, hovers crimson-eyed at the abyss.
The man's shadow shuffles behind the walker
like slow ferris wheels into the haze of evening.

She drives her damp saline face to visit, broods
over pressure spikes, reads to him, tells jokes,
bends down to know that he still breathes.
You wish you could stop listening...

Watching

Stroke survivor, you lie there,
contorted in repose, legs asprawl,
yellowed ivory concealed
in your gaping mouth,
arms folded like marble statues
of saints, meditating martyrdom.

Your plaid-encased chest arrests
my eyes, my face frozen in frown.
Eons stagger by. Lot's wife,
I stand rigid, crystalline. I hold
my breath as I watch for signs
of yours.

Fear of Abandonment,

of imminent widowhood,
gnaws at the core of my being,
destroys any hope of serenity.

The future haunts my present
as I await the sweep of the scythe
through my husband's
stooped vulnerability.

Post Stroke

The first fall drops him floorward,
no outward sign of bruise, no break.
His confidence cracked, the cane
becomes a constant companion.

Edema balloons his feet and legs.
Inflated limbs, crimson-angry,
seek to burst their dermal bonds,
shoes unfitting, socks strangle.

Speech slows, tone diminishes,
inflection high-pitched, childlike.
Vision improves but stays double.
Depth perception diminishes.

Dismal side effects vie
with medication changes.
Stamina, a wistful memory, walking,
a battle as wayward left leg hugs gravity.

Hope

Therapists trundle the stroke
survivors into their vehicle
to tour a nearby orchard.
In silence the group waits—
many with arms frozen into
positions of uselessness,
legs braced with steel and plastic,
heads cocked in query pose,
eyelids drooping, tongues thwarted
in desperate struggle for coherency.

The wife of one sees them off,
visualizes a basket of vegetables,
misshapen, withered, bent over,
being carted away. Feintly smiling,
she wafts a *have-fun* wave
as the van disappears,
then wipes her eyes, blows her nose,
muses: *It's not too bad.*
Broken carrots, split tomatoes,
sprouted potatoes, still make
a damned good stew.

When I Am Dead

When I am dead, my dearest,
who will conclude your sentences for you?

Who will assist you to retrieve
words hidden in oblivion?

Who will help you cope with the universe,
find your gloves, buy the right toothpaste?

Who will rage about the decibel overload
with which you fill our house?

Who will wake you from those
horrific nightmares?

Who will shower you with endless quips,
quirky puns?

Who will defy your philosophy of learning,
resist it to the end?

Who will remind you where you are heading,
maybe even why?

If you need my help with all the above,
I shall come back and do my best, my love.

You will neither see nor hear me clearly,
but I shall be there. I love you dearly.

Resonance

Over forty years, I have stood
atop a hill on five acres
of windswept land, my life
resonating with the lives
of my aged inhabitants. In spirit
and physicality we are intertwined,
mirroring the effect of the depredation
of time on all of us.

When I first met the couple,
they walked straight and tall.
Now their spines echo the ruptures
in my root-distorted driveway.
Their thin and whitened hair is like
my shingles, battered by wind and rain.
His prostate cancer, her incontinence,
reflect the abrupt malfunction
of my venerable septic system.

The erratic hesitation of my furnace
in deepest winter parallels her spate
of weak spells and palpitations.
Their old joints stiffen in arthritic
lock step as my joists start to sag.
The care of my lawn is now entrusted
to strangers. Weeds challenge
the diminished garden beds.
My gutters droop and weep.

Each night we three commune, wonder
whether all of us will crash together,
worn-out creatures, carted away, grist
for new buildings, new life forms.

Reunion

A smile creeps across her aged face
as she greets three generations of offspring
drawn by the magnet of her money
to an annual family get together.

They feign love and devotion
smothering her with the saga
of broken furnaces, worn-out roofs,
failed businesses and needed tuition aid.

As she imagines the reading of her will,
each one receiving one silver dollar,
her five cats inheriting the rest,
a smile creeps across her aged face.

Pretzels,

entwined, brittle, salt-bedecked,
how well they serve as metaphor

for next-door neighbor's brain,
salted with plaques and tangles,
her memory, mind, humanity
inexorably dissolving, evaporating

for intersections of land-devouring
concrete, bends, turns, overlaps,
salted with drivers frantically
rushing from here to where

for posture of octogenarians,
cantilevered, twisted, fighting
gravity, brittle bones defying
falls, hair whiter than salt

She Has Left Us

Birds pause in their flight to winter haven,
dip a wing in farewell to one
who has left us in her 91st year.

Shadows veil the light, wind hushes
the air, tears of the hidden sun
moisten her untended garden bed.
Mundane memories turn sacred;
her remaining possessions morph
with grace into relics.

The soft, chirpy voice heard for decades
is stilled. Her touch is beyond our reach.
Her going was not unexpected,
leaves a deep eddy in familial waters.
Friends and relatives struggle to change
tenses when they mention her. Other hands
will tend her garden, dust her things.

Spring

I survive with panache the weight
  of bone-shivering frost, dearth of daylight.

April, battered by days of freezing wind,
  weeps against my window pane.

Promise of verdant resurrection frees my eyes
  from a spectrum of gray, white, brown.

Oak-tall, I stand stretching my limbs
  in anticipation of floral color, fragrance.

Grateful for their past embrace,
  I shed scarf, gloves, quilted coat.

Winter-withered, my friends are gone,
  and I alone can welcome spring.

In the Plaza

Sultry flamenco dancers twist
in scarlet swirls; their flashing
feet beat a feral rhythm. Dark men
twang guitars in a frenzy of wails,
lamenting their lost love.

The Seville sun gleams off
silver buttons and gold
tassels that adorn the uniform
of a handsome soldier,
whom the dancer brazenly seduces.

Crescendos of trumpets
herald the crowd hailing
a proud, slender toreador,
bull slayer, lady killer,
the fickle filly's latest target.

One Afternoon in June

Seductive, eerie to western ears,
music of Lebanon, Egypt, Turkey,
fills the festival plaza. Incessant
percussion, wailing voices excite
dance troop and eager audience.

Sequin glitter, dangle of beads,
coins jingling on hip scarves--
a dozen sinuous women and girls,
wear yards of translucent
fabric, whirl and undulate.

In supple slippers of silver and gold,
midriffs bare below brazen bras,
they pulsate over flashing low-slung
skirts, harem pants of luscious
turquoise, jade, deep rose.
.
And who is that familiar figure
wriggling way off beat, ample hips
in staccato motion, wildly wafting
Sumo-heavy arms, gyrating
an ancient, golden-bell-clad rear,

her scarlet face panting
for oxygen, eyes ecstatic strobe
lights? Holy cow! Out there,
before the cheering crowds,
our Grandma shakes and shimmies!

Shall We Dance

Dear Mom, don't laugh.
I'm learning to belly dance!
Picture me, 190-pound klutz, grey hair,
arthritic knees, clad in glittering diaphanous
blue-green harem pants topped by a black sports
bra (non-existent in your time). Gold necklaces
and chains of small ringing bells lie on my chest,
sequined green bracelets adorn my wrists,
and dangling earrings frame my sagging face.
Best of all, around my hips I tie a sleek shawl
with rows of glittering gold coins
that jingle and flash as I move.

When you see me dance, Mom,
(almost to the beat of the music),
you'll smile, cry or redden in embarrassment
as I get carried away by the exotic rhythms.
My rusty joints, skimpy stamina belie the effort
to seem sinuous and seductive
while isolated parts of my body try to gyrate.

If we could meet again, you with eyesight restored,
both of us forty years younger, thirty pounds lighter,
I'd give you a very special demonstration.
Maybe you'd join in. I miss you.

 Love, Annette

Voluptuous

Coiled with desire,
snake embraces
undulating neck and arm
of poet as she dances.
Supple body garbed in waves
of glittering opulence--
orchid, gold, green, rose,
turquoise--over royal-
purple palpitating
belly. Ebony eyes glint,
entice, threaten, as
scarlet tongue hisses
its serpentine song. Poet
dances on, undaunted by
decision snake must make:
Caress or strike?

Two Fires

Cheers and song arose from
the joyous crowds celebrating
the coming of age of their beloved
daughters. An aura of affection
and warmth infused everyone at
the ceremony, centered around
a blazing bonfire. Breeze-blown reeds
in the flickering light, the young women
swayed with rhythmic grace as
they danced away their childhood.

In the 31st Girls Middle School in Mecca,
fourteen young women were murdered.
A fire broke out in the school and hundreds
of panicked students raced for an exit.
The Committee for the Propagation
of Virtue and the Prevention of Vice
blocked one gate, refusing access to
rescuers, firefighters, paramedics.
The fourteen were not wearing
the mandatory Islamic garb.
Their hair was uncovered,
their dresses too short.

Flight

The pterodactyl, last of its kind,
drifted above the germs of the future--
dolphins, alligators, canaries, humans.
A life in free fall, its cries beckoned.
The crescendo of choked caws
and flap of faltering limbs
vaporized in a wingéd timewarp.

Vitreous Universe

Twin darkish orbs dominate
planar matrix of mini bubbles:
sinister eyes or captive nano worlds.

Stark bundles of floral stalks,
slate-blue heads sans petals,
sepals, leaves, encapsulated
in transparent swirls of
aqua, green, anemic blue.

The whole, a densely-weighted,
flat-bottomed spherical dome,
forming stemless mushroom:
phantom fungus of the future.
Evolution frozen in glass?

Explosion of Dragons

Wet-on-wet merging of watery hues.
Colors flaunt their attributes,
overtake and intermingle,
assimilate edges,
reds into oranges, blues into purples,
create intense sunset/sunrise.
Blue-black writhing network
silhouetted against sky.
Tails, talons, tongues,
horns, hearts, heads
expanding, contracting.
An explosion of dragons.

Define Me

Room upon room of disorder defines me,
not quite chaotic, merely free-formed:
layered fossils of domestic litter,
mini-eons of dust-kissed papers,
delicate traces of feline hair clumps,
discontinuities of half-finished tasks,
sinkholes of unsorted laundry,
eruptions of overflowing waste baskets,
avalanches of unread magazines,
tar beds of procrastination.

I Sing a Song to Singer,

the black and gold machine
with its guillotine needle
and dastardly bobbins.

Why, O toy of the devil,
did you choose to torment
me from the age thirteen?

Some are destined to sew
and others like me to rip
and pucker and snarl, break

needles, blow fuses, set
sleeves in backwards, stitch
zippers shut. Your needles

refused to let me feed them.
The seams I sewed on you
seemed so unseemly.

I should have traded you
in for a hammer, a screw
driver, a wrench, a saber saw;

but given my dearth of dexterity
dealing with any device,
my defeat would soon ensue.

So I sing to you, great stitcher,
a song of forgiveness and farewell,
for computers form my newest hell.

Lost in the Font

I wander through cyberspace
searching for myself.
A clumsy click and I'm whisked
from an incipient poem
exalting the visual appeal
of alphabetic shapes.

I yearn for an exotic style
to enhance my words,
relying on form instead of content.
Save me. I am lost in the font.

Whenever

I sit at my desk and try to squeeze a poem
from the mass of neurons in my head.
I have exhausted lines about personal loss,
ill health, the tedium of ageing. To extol
love of country, gush over nature
or praise an invisible god repels me,
or at least puts me off. I hunger
for subject matter to put my teeth into,
chew with eloquence, swallow with self-
satisfaction, savor with pride. Nothing comes.

My pen—robust, juicy, eager to perform—
regards me in despair. My piece of paper
looks up blankly, in hope of fulfillment. Sorry,
friends, no mission, no spark, no syllable for you.
Maybe tomorrow, next Thursday, whenever.

French Critic

On Elba, Napoleon Bonaparte
tore an English poem apart.
Sacrebleu! He parsed, he scanned, he read aloud.
(For this task, the general had no heart.)
Mon Dieu! These verses make no sense.
The Anglais hitch the horse behind the cart.
Their rhythm is off, their rhymes are merde.
They're not worth a Frenchman's fart.

Picture George

George Washington crosses the Delaware
standing erect, a human bowsprit.
Must we entrust our new nation
to such an unnautical twit?

Tattered, tired men toil at their oars
fearing old George will swamp them of course.
At the least, this leader of the brave and free
could lower his butt, pull hard for liberty.

Music

Seven erudite crocodiles
cascaded ashore in ecstasy
astride the triumphant tsunami.
Their voices sanctified the raging seas,
crystallized all into a soaring oratorio,
the score cannibalized from "*La Mer.*"

Cell Phone World

People stride along downtown
face contorted with deep frown,
hand held to ear, speaking bold.
A hundred thousand living
soap operas publicly unfold:

*I'm crossing State Street now, against
the light. Oops, he almost hit me.
I'm out of the good rubbers.
I'll get some, and then come right...*

*Feed the cat. Lock the door
and don't forget your appointment
with the shrink. I can't stand
another night with you wanting to...*

*I couldn't care less! I did what I
can to stop her before she really
screws herself and us with that...*

*After the lights went out, he pushed
me down onto the laundry basket
and put his hot, greasy hands on my...*

*He promised me that it wouldn't
make a difference. What a frigging liar!
Now I can't even...*

*Of course, it's all your fault.
After all the times we've done it,
you never seem to learn.
Just wait until I'm ready to...*

Ten Chosen Words

A cinnamon encounter
enthralls in aromatic ways,
but saffron interpolates
among shimmering auroras
and loquacious mandibles.
I vegetate in anticipation.

Waiting

> *My letters are bird tracks in the sand.*
> *"The Refugees" – Barbara Crooker*

Forty-seven days, still no response.
(I typed the last letter to provide clarity.)
My handwriting "puzzles" you, you say,
like a blur of mist, the sprawl of Sanskrit.

But how can the meaning elude you,
my words succinct, blunt, tear-stained?
Perhaps you lack ink or paper, a stamp.
Receiving a negative reply would erase

the winter of no answer at all. I breathe,
I eat, but my life is suspended between
your final words and the silence of
indifference. Mercy. Mercy. Please write.

Ashes on Snow

Diverse blacks, tinged with gray,
layered remnant of burnt letters,
bills, ads, pleas for money.
Sooty, fragile, wind-kissed,
left in woods atop unbroken snow.
Mirror of oriental art,
subtle values, delicate lines,
hint of secret tragedy.

Jelly Beans

A tall jar half full of ovoid shapes sits on a barrel head in the poet's living room. Each jelly bean in the glass container displays a vivid color, contrasting and harmonizing with its haphazardly-stacked neighbors, the brilliant hues belying the secrets they conceal. The single scarlet bean reflects in sequence blood aboil in ardor and blood spilt in anger. Its intense cinnamon flavor sears both memories into the tongue. Bright orange beans recall a sunlit tropical afternoon redolent with the perfume of citrus, through which a lone winsome woman wanders. Pearlescent white pieces hark back to youthful weddings where innocent brides are enveloped in the bittersweetness of the nuptial bed. A few beans lurk in sinister black, their sonorous scent of licorice evoking life's somber grief.

Congratulations on Your Affair

Here's cayenne in the eye,
fishbone in the throat,
glass ground in the bread,
Drano in the soup.

Domestic Scene

The wife, bent over
from years of strife,
dreamed of kinder life,
free of verbal thrashing,
implied violence.
She prepared the supper
he demanded, cutting
mushrooms, onions, sausages
with her twelve-inch kitchen knife.
Gleaming in the moving blade,
her dear dead mother's face
appeared and whispered:
When he's asleep, really slice.

Presents

Receiving, infinitely more
painful than giving, wants
acknowledgement, feigned gratitude.

Utter: *How lovely! Thank you.*
Think: *Where did she find that
monstrosity?*

Say: *Oh this will match my
new sofa.*
Opine in silence: *I'll put it out
only when I know you are coming.*

Voice: *I've always wanted
a jeweled can opener.*
Feel: *Is she trying to tell
me something?*

Verbalize: *Thank you for the silky
bra embroidered with crimson A's.*
Realize: *She knows about me and
Jonathan!*

Teaching a Stone to Talk

In my youth I found a strange
and jagged stone. I held it in my hand,
felt a calling to teach and nurture it.

I bathed it in cool, fresh water
to cleanse its inhibition. I let
the sun sparkle on its many facets.

I surrounded the stone with fragrant
flowers, lilacs and lilies of the valley,
to enhance its senses.

In a sonorous voice, I read it poems
about its mountain forebears
and the sands of its future progeny.

To impart a noble vocabulary,
I spoke to it for years in words
of Shakespeare, Dante, King James.

I tendered a flickering candle
to serve as a teacher in the night,
show how it could change and glow.

I painted its portrait larger
than life to acknowledge
and celebrate its intricate shape.

I kept the stone with me in a silent place,
caressed it with loving kisses.
At last, it spoke, rasped: *Buzz off, lady!*

I have wasted my whole life.

Time Taunts

The past floats
across my blank eyes.
The present teases me,
promises, shows,
then withholds.
The future, illusive,
fragmented, beckons,
fades, deserts. Despair
and comfort alternate,
slowly sucking me
into time's vacuum.

Last Call

Long have I lived and seen a lot,
am loath to go when I am called.
Began life shoeless, without pot.
Long have I lived and seen a lot.
Parted I'll be from all I've got,
carted from here, no teeth, quite bald.
Long have I lived and seen a lot,
am loath to go when I am called.

Afterwards

With certainty death gives birth to closure,
complete oblivion, unbroken slumber,
sensual shutdown, cessation of process,
dearth of movement.

Mind/soul/spirit evanesces,
awareness vanishes,
body begins redefining itself.
Molecules assume new roles.

Reincarnation possible,
except for memory.
Not ours the choice
in which form we return:

bird, spoon, geranium,
chewing gum, el Niño, uranium,
flu virus, kangaroo, golden ring,
tsetse fly, leper, a rusty swing.

Memories

Memory resides on a spider web
woven round and round on sticky spokes.
Old events cling to the spiral,
a few fixed for the long run,
others dangle by a thread.

My web is now hole-ridden,
torn and missing strands,
what once adhered, gone.
Pleasant memories, painful recollections,
most dissolved in temporal mists.
Ends of stories dry up, lose their grip,
beginnings barely hang on.

Was I ever spanked? Enough to cry?
What happened to my beloved raincoats,
the deep purple one with its yards and yards
of flowing fabric, the pale blue one fashioned
for a general? Who was the first man I
dared to kiss? Did I enjoy it? Did I ever
speak with my mother's mother? Who
tried to rape me on a blind date?

Ugly events and embarrassments persist;
the glowing moments all disappeared.
I shall know all the answers and many more
when I, too, am but a memory.

Pearls

My life is a length
of unmatched pearls
strung on a fraying thread.
No bead of tranquility lies
along the lustrous strand.
Self-made stress and neuroses
corrode the glimmering orbs.
Soon the thread will fail,
the pearls drop, scatter,
and inexorably roll back
to the sea that spawned them.

When

is the proper moment to go,
to depart from where I am,
book passage to soft
oblivion?

How weary of body
and fearful of soul
must I feel to justify,
before chance-ordained time,
the inevitable journey?

How do I prepare for leaving--
advise family and friends--
or simply elope in silence?
The vehicle that takes me
must be fail-safe,
no round-trip ticket wanted.

I ponder the last decision,
not if, just when and how.

Passing Through

I believe neither in heaven
nor hell, nor other destination.
Like a night train, whistle muted,
I pass with little fanfare
through here to there to nowhere.
Nevertheless I ponder
what to carry with me
for my eons of oblivion.

Poems by Billy Collins,
Verdi operas, Mozart's *Requiem,*
a bouquet of O'Keeffe's flowers,
the aroma of Thai restaurants,
the sinuous silhouettes of our cats,
the intoxication of chocolate,
my husband's soft voice and smile.

I have no ticket, but my bags are packed.
I await the conductor's call.

The Black Door

I go through the red door, smell roses,
watch a cardinal, start bleeding.

I go through the green door, become
motion sick, eat spinach, feel jealous.

I go through the blue door, begin
to shiver, become morose, drip ink.

I go through the yellow door, slip
on butter, grow afraid, hear canaries.

I go through the purple door, drink
wine, paint an eggplant, feel passionate.

I go through the orange door, sip
screw drivers, carve pumpkins, shred carrots.

I go through the black door, mourn
my dead brother, go blind, lose my memory.

Meditation

Insomnia is my meditation.
In the dark I squiggle and squirm,
trivial thoughts are inhaled,
dire thoughts are exhaled.
The slumber bird wings aloft,
seeks a pathway in. But no piece
of peace flies out. Minute matters
wax urgent, reiterate, rut
into my brain. Hours melt by.
The clock jeers that I will
never sleep again.

Sole-Stirring Night

I dream of mud, cool, squishy, oozing
between my toes, awakening dark
scenes of childhood—a mixture
of shameful dirt and inadvertent tears.
For days I limp along, struggle not
to lose my balance and to prevent
the sinister muck from sucking
up my hopeless, helpless existence.

I fantasize about being partially
barefoot—one shoe missing—
trudging through twenty degree
snow, my unshod foot burning
in the damp cold, then going numb,
turning the color of dead embers.

Thank You, Dad,

for my lack of dancing skill,
my reticence to show affection,
my tendency towards diabetes,
my throwing off of religion,
my playing second fiddle to your son,
my overblown sense of honesty,
my rigid work ethic,
my unforgiving conscience,
my lack of common vices.

William Beane: Redwing, 1888

I do not know or really care who William Beane was. Seeing his name as the title and subject of someone's poem brought to mind my recently deceased younger brother, Harris Bernard Siegel. From earliest time, he was cursed with the nickname Beanie. The story told by the family was that he was so skinny at birth that he resembled a string bean, hence Beanie. We never thought much about the name beyond the fact that that was what we called him. Seventy years later, I learned to my surprise that he had always loathed the name. Not until he was in his fifties did he have the self-confidence to insist that everyone refer to and address him as Harry. I loved the name Harris, but he considered it too pretentious and perhaps even a bit effeminate. Beanie stammered through an unhappy childhood with a speech impediment, protruding upper teeth, and a jealous, harassing older sister. Very intelligent, he never was able to avail himself of formal education. He had very few friends, two unhappy marriages, no children, and no interests beyond his water-softening business. Beanie endured loss of a kidney and several heart attacks. Suspected malpractice killed him when he became riddled with massive infection following emergency surgery. My brother left shocked relatives an estate in the millions.

Call

me, please, right now,
the moment you open this.
My sleep is fractured,
my hunger in flight.
Your final words,
so very terse, so sparse,
darkly toll your departure.

I implore you to forgive
the unforgivable, forget
that which should be forgotten.

My eyes are arid, exhausted of tears.
A word, a syllable, a hint of hope
is all I need to salvage my soul,
bolster my body. Have pity,
compassion, mercy in the name
of what once was ours.

Mood Indigo

I'm still in the mood, Indigo, loving you,
feeling lonely, so forlorn, so blue.
Indigo, you left me without hope, quite nude,
Crushing this loyal, doting dude.
That wasn't a merciful way to go.
Help me revive that mood, Indigo.

Glitter

Thanks to Barbara Crooker's "Glitter"

The first time it happened,
I expected my blood to turn
fizzy, to gaze at silver stars,
hear harps and bells and trumpets.

Lying on sheets of black and navy,
in a January too cold for birds,
I watched the headlight beams
pierce the dullness of the ceiling

and wondered: Is this it? That's all?
For this I guarded my treasure,
counted the days and hours till I bared it?
What was God doing? She promised me glitter.

Romantic Reverie

George, you bastard, why did you let me believe you were single?

David, you were so inept, so clueless about how deep you hurt me, never even aware of it.

Roberto, you shit, you just wanted me to be your American fiancée to qualify for a green card.

Larry, you misled me for months. I was too innocent to recognize your bisexuality.

OK, guys, listen up. Don't compare notes or attempt to apologize. Just realize you couldn't pull that crap on me today.

I don't care if it is cold and raining and near midnight. I'm dumping the sorry lot of you at the next truck stop.

Doing It

Last night I didn't, but I could have, should have, probably would have, but lacked strength, moral courage, sufficient time. Better planning, proper preparation, positive determination might have made a difference. OK, OK, once more into the breach...

Tonight I'll approach it obliquely, not pretend fatigue or disinterest. I will repeat my new mantra: *Yes I must. Yes I shall. Yes I must. Yes I shall.* It might work if I try hard enough. I really intend to do it. No more procrastination or weak excuses. Yes I must! Yes I shall!

Yes I did it! Before going to bed, I flossed my seven remaining teeth.

Ignis

Fuego, feu, feuer, fire,
symbol of danger, resentment,
contentment, ardor, anger, heat.

Creator of smoke--black, gray, white--
billowing, choking, blinding,
warning, signaling, enticing

with smell of camp fire, incense,
grilled beef, scented candle, marijuana.
Fuego, feu, feuer, fire.

What I Put Into The Bag

My favorite bag with its pink and chartreuse abstract design, accented with black piping and black straps, accompanies me everywhere. It is like really no one's business what I put in the bag when I go to my middle school class or attend those great parties with my brother's college friends. I scorn facial paint but do rely on Mom's best cologne to create an aura of worldliness I have yet to earn. Oh, yes, the bag. Depending on the occasion, along with comb, mirror, cell phone, house key, Bic pen and short pencil, Kleenex, plastic water bottle, and wallet containing too few dollars, I put in three tampons, five condoms in their original container, a pack of cigarettes with lighter, two Twinkies, some trail gorp, and my good-luck fuzzy stuffed penguin. On the top of these essentials, I put in a school book or two and a thin notebook to ward off inquisitive parental eyes.

Numbers

What's in a number?
Why are some more significant,
more powerful than others?
Who ascribed characteristics
to certain numbers?
What do repeating patterns
of numbers connote?
(Consider poor pi, spewing
numbers into infinity.)
Who identified 666
with evil, the devil?
Why do buildings avoid
numbering their 13th floor?
Wherefore does three represent
the Christian god, describe
the parts of Gaul, and determine
the totality of grantable wishes?
How do we set the age
for passage to adulthood—
thirteen, fifteen, eighteen, twenty-one?
Explain three Furies, four
corners to the earth, five senses,
ten commandments, twenty-four
hours? Why does seventh heaven
exceed the bliss of the first six?

Dragon's Tale

Enclosed in flask with cap of gold
a scent emerged, redolent of old
and fearsome dragons who bled
from tail and wings and head.
Their blood not scarlet but yellowish green
coursed through heart and liver, lastly spleen.
With each threat of talons and burst of flame
the more evanescent its scent became
until one day at appearance of dawn
both gentle scent and dragon were gone.

Clangor

I love you all, bongo, bass, tympani,
pulsating heartbeat of a symphony,
triangle, glockenspiel, marimba, snare,
cymbal, tambourine, bells--all I hear.

Slide me a trombone, a bugle, a fife,
sound aglitter like a golden knife.
A trumpet, a tuba, a flute, all brass,
calling to arms, to victory, to mass.

Forget the strings and most of the reeds,
not stirring enough to suit my needs.
Blending the brass with the beat of drums,
I immerse my spirit in whatever comes.